AUTHOR & FINISHER OF MY FAITH

by

Winifred Smith Eure

10 INSPIRATIONAL POEMS

Print information available on the last page

Rev. date: 02/10/2016

To order additional copies of this book, contact:
Xlibris
1-888-795-4274
www.Xlibris.com
Orders@Xlibris.com

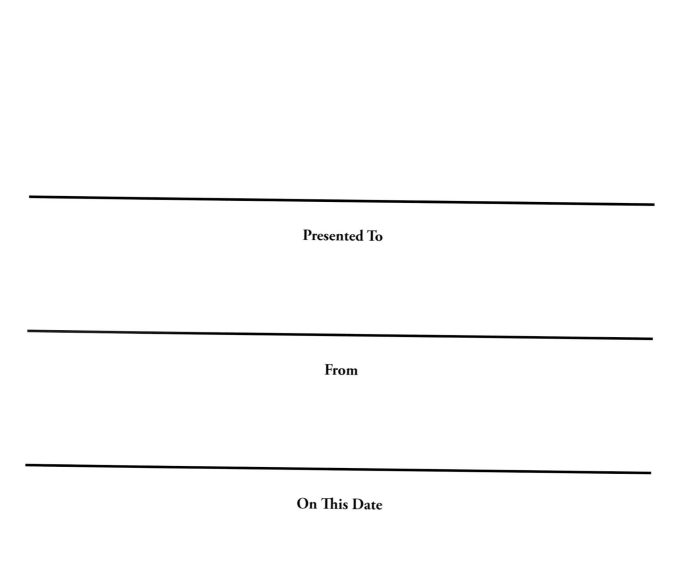

Presented To

From

On This Date

INTRODUCTION

I know the Savior as a Way-Maker . I am an author because He is the Author and Finisher of My Faith.

Whoever said "Tough times make tough people" was right. Most of my adult life I've known people to whom this applies.

If I had to leave some words of advice and encouragement to the younger generations, I would repeat these words: Put God first in your life and all other things will follow. "Dare to dream, but be more than a dreamer." Remember, Faith without works is dead. (James 2:17 NIV)

Perhaps there is something written here in these poems that will help you in times of adversity. Let Jesus come into your heart!

DEDICATION

This book is dedicated to all of my family and friends. O taste and see that the Lord is good: blessed is the one who takes refuge in Him. (Psalm 34:8)

CONTENTS

Introduction   3

Dedication   5

Contents   7

God Is . . .   8

Simply Because   10

Sleeping with the Enemy?   11

My Father, My Friend   12

Have Thine Own Way   14

For Every Believer   16

After God's Own Heart   17

My Redeemer   18

My Daily Prayer For You
(Heard Church Family)   19

Arrived?   20

God Is . . .

God is the sparkle in a child's eye.
God is the flavor in Grandma's sweet potato pie.
God is the perennial green of grass and plants.
God is the warmth of springtime.
God is the silent prayers of married couples.
God is the house built on a firm foundation.
God is the tears in a mother's cry for her wayward child.
God is the doctor when yours has given up hope.
God is the peace that follows fervent prayer.
God is the joy that cometh after a night of weeping.
God is the rainbow after the rain.
God is the Jesus in you and me.

Simply Because

Simply because
I was once young too,
young people, I want to leave
this message with you.

Whatever be your hopes and dreams,
pray and persevere.
Don't be distracted
by discouragement or occasional tears.

Jesus loves you
and will lead and guide.
Be humble always
not puffed up with pride.

Sure you'll make mistakes
along the way.
You may be tempted
to go astray.

Your friends forsake you.
Your enemies draw nigh.
But the grace of God
will abide.

He'll protect
and keep you near,
if you trust Him
above your peers.

Don't fear hard work.
Don't cave in to hindrances.
Both could turn out to be among
your sweetest remembrances.

And when that day comes
it's love you're searching for,
first look to God.
He is the open door.

Sleeping with the Enemy?

Worry, hate and fear
are emotions that should have
no place here
in our lives.

For they wreak havoc
in body, mind and soul
and keep us from
being whole.

They rob us from
inner sanctity
until we lose
our trust in Thee, Heavenly Father.

Yes, worry, hate and fear
don't house them
in this New Year.
Instead, hold fast to hope, faith and love.

My Father, My Friend

If Jesus were here
with me today
we'd walk along
the roadside way.
I'd tell Him
how happy I am
to have found
a friend in Him.
I'd confide
my deepest thoughts,
tell Him
everything I ought.
Follow His lead
oh so true,
be blessed by Him
through and through.
My Father in heaven
dearest to me
I yield, I believe.
I trust in Thee.

Have Thine Own Way

Dear Father,
Sometimes I enjoy when it rains.
I sit back in my favorite chair and bask in the
unique peace that surrounds me.
A perfect calm
overshadows any doubt and fear and
I live in the stillness of the moment.
My heart bubbles over with sheer joy
as I wonder at your marvelous work
watering the trees, plants and grass.
You prepare us for new growth as
the earth is washed and made clean.
I rise from a holy place within and envision
a spiritual mountain where I can look out
and feel blessed to see abundant life and newness.
Nothing is greater than You most merciful Father.
Your vastness is insurmountable and your
height, width and depth unreachable.
Have Thine own way, Lord.

For Every Believer

IT WAS something more than earthly rule
that paid our debt of sin in full.

It was more than the angels and prophecy
that prepared the way for you and me.

It was more than baby Jesus' birth
that decided every human's worth.

It was more than frankincense, myrrh, and gold
that created the greatest story ever told.

It was more than teaching, miracles, and healing
that inspired a following with ardent feeling.

It was more than lamentations and tears
that calmed our doubts and diminished our fears.

It was the ultimate sacrifice, the cross, THE
RESURRECTION
that ignited our hope, our eternal life connection.

IT IS more than hearts of song and care
that equips us with faith so rare.

It is more than increase and gain
that walks us through the stormy rain.

It is more than creation's day and night
that encourages returning to the light.

It is more than what Christians have heard.
It's how we apply the scriptures, the truth, the Word.

It is more than our own good works,
but divine intervention with God's masterworks.

It is the highest calling
that keeps us from falling.

It's Jesus! the ALPHA and OMEGA
who provides for every believer.

After God's Own Heart

He called my loved one home.
My heart ached on my own.
I dare not try to replace or act in
conscious haste
to know another's soul to have man
and to hold.
When I came to my sense
it mattered what God replenished.
I sought my God indeed
and tried His word to heed.
My life I gave to Him.
His heart I want to win -
that He should grant me grace
and bless me as I pace
my steps in Him alone
until He calls me home.
I bid His face to see
and hope He welcomes me
to Heaven up above.
It's Jesus that I love.

My Redeemer

I know that my Redeemer lives
for He has etched upon my heart my own story,
a light replacing darkness,
love filling the emptiness, a flower grown from
its roots, and today I murmur a thousand
thank yous for His having lifted me from
despair and inspired within a hope and faith that
endures.
Yes, I know that my Redeemer lives. I
feel His presence all about me, in my
attitude and every endeavor. Surely His
hand is forever near. I revere and need Him
without end.
Yes, I know that my Redeemer lives.

My Daily Prayer For You
(Heard Church Family)

From refreshing sweet dreams
To morning grace
To afternoon peace
To evening joy
This is my daily prayer for you.

From God's bountiful love
To familial thanksgiving
To friendship's sharing
To neighbors' respect
This is my daily prayer for you.

From the precious blood of Jesus
To the end of warring nations
To the ceasing of street crime and violence
To the breaking down of all barriers to racial harmony
This is my daily prayer for you.

From the truth of His Word
To the light of your minds
To the courage of your presence
To the boldness of your feet
This is my daily prayer for you.

May God wrap His arms around you
In your going out and in your coming in.
Amen.

Arrived?

Out of slavery and oppression
into the bleak days and nights
of subtle racism and discrimination
drafted by robust winds of segregation
in housing and education
faced with the harsh reality of unemployment
and the false security of welfare
reared by our spiritual leaders, community activists,
and awesome teachers
rising through the ranks of faith, good works,
and disciplined education
God loved us when we
couldn't love ourselves enough.
We were raised by the blood of Jesus
and power of His holy name.
We've become a people of a revered and coveted grace.
But has Martin's dream and Malcolm's epiphany
ARRIVED?

Printed in the United States
By Bookmasters